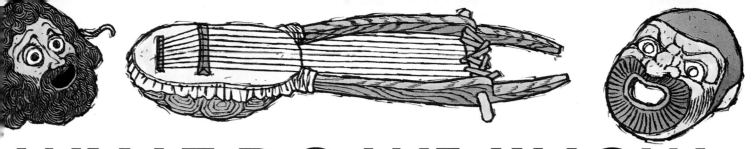

WHAT·DO·WE·KNOW
ABOUT  THE
GREEKS·?

ANNE PEARSON

PETER BEDRICK BOOKS
NEW YORK

First American edition published in 1992 by
Peter Bedrick Books
2112 Broadway
New York, NY 10023

Published by agreement with Simon & Schuster Young Books, Hemel Hempstead, England

Library of Congress Cataloging-in-Publication Data
Pearson. Anne.
    What do we know about the Greeks?/Anne Pearson. – 1st American ed.
    Includes index.
    Summary: Surveys the eating habits, education, housing,
recreation, religion, art, and other aspects of life in ancient Greece.
    ISBN 0–87226–356–8
    1. Greece–Civilization–To 146 B.C.–Juvenile literature.
(1. Greece–Civilization–To 146 B.C.)   I. Title.
DF77.P365   1992   92–9692
938–dc20   CIP
                                                            AC

Design: David West
            Children's Book Design

Illustrator: Rob Shone

Copy editor: Ros Mair

Photograph acknowledgements: The Ancient Art & Architecture Collection: p16(b), p17(t),
p25(b), p30(both), p31, p39, p43(tr); Archiv Fur Kunst und Geschichte Berlin/Erich Lessing:
p13(b), p16(t); Courtesy The Ashmolean Museum: p21(b); The Trustees of the British
Museum; endpapers, p8(t), p12, p15(t), p17(both), p19(both) p20, p21(t), p23, p33(l), p41;
C.M. Dixon: p13(t), p22(both), p36–7; Werner Forman Archive: p24(b); Michael Holford:
cover p8(b), p9, p14, p24(t), p25(t), p26(both), p27(all), p28(both), p29(t), p32, p33(r),
p34(both), p35(both), p37(tl, and tr), p38, p40, p42, p43(tl), p43(b); Courtesy The National
Tourist Organisation of Greece: p29(b); Courtesy Wurzburg Museum: p15(b).

Picture research: Jennie Karrach

Typeset by: Goodfellow and Egan, Cambridge

Printed and bound by: BPCC Hazell Books, Paulton
and Aylesbury, England.

· CONTENTS ·

WHO WERE THE GREEKS?	8
TIMELINE	10
WHERE DID THE GREEKS GET THEIR FOOD?	12
DID THE GREEKS EAT WELL?	14
DID THE GREEKS HAVE FAMILIES LIKE OURS?	16
DID THE GREEKS LIVE IN HOUSES?	18
DID BOYS AND GIRLS GO TO SCHOOL?	20
WHO WENT TO WORK IN GREEK TIMES?	22
WHAT DID THE GREEKS DO IN THEIR SPARE TIME?	24
WHAT DID THE GREEKS WEAR?	26
WHO DID THE GREEKS WORSHIP?	28
DID THE GREEKS GO TO THE DOCTOR?	30
WHO RULED THE GREEKS?	32
WERE THE GREEKS ARTISTS?	34
DID THE GREEKS GO TO THE THEATER?	36
WERE THE GREEKS SCIENTISTS?	38
DID THE GREEKS GO ON LONG JOURNEYS?	40
WHAT WAS LIFE LIKE IN THE ARMY?	42
GLOSSARY	44
INDEX	45

WHO·WERE ·THE· GREEKS?

Ancient Greece was never one united country. Although the Greeks spoke the same language and called themselves Greeks, they belonged to a number of little city-states, each with its own main town, government, army and coinage. The cities competed with one another for land and trade. Because the land of Greece was so barren, many Greeks emigrated to new colonies, in Asia Minor and all over the Mediterranean.

THE ACROPOLIS

Other city-states paid money to Athens to defend them if they were attacked. This money contributed to Athenian wealth and was used to build the great temples on the Acropolis, shown below. This great rock was a fortress at times of war, and gradually emerged as the religious center of the city.

LIFE IN ATHENS

In the fifth century BC, the city-state of Athens reached the height of her power and Athenians lived in peace and prosperity. The scenes on the many vases made in Athens, like the one on the right, show a luxurious lifestyle, with Greeks reclining on fine couches, listening to music. Athens became a great center of learning and art. Many famous Greeks lived there.

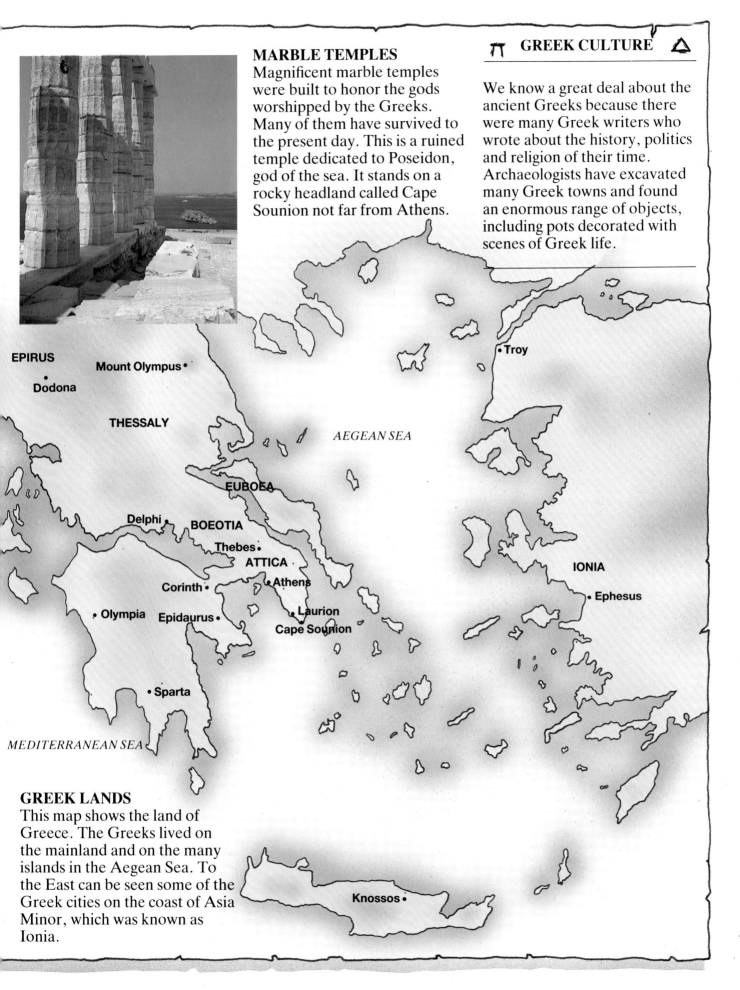

MARBLE TEMPLES

Magnificent marble temples were built to honor the gods worshipped by the Greeks. Many of them have survived to the present day. This is a ruined temple dedicated to Poseidon, god of the sea. It stands on a rocky headland called Cape Sounion not far from Athens.

We know a great deal about the ancient Greeks because there were many Greek writers who wrote about the history, politics and religion of their time. Archaeologists have excavated many Greek towns and found an enormous range of objects, including pots decorated with scenes of Greek life.

EPIRUS

Mount Olympus •

• Dodona

THESSALY

AEGEAN SEA

• Troy

EUBOEA

Delphi •

BOEOTIA

Thebes •

ATTICA

Corinth •

• Athens

IONIA

• Ephesus

• Olympia

Epidaurus •

• Laurion

Cape Sounion

• Sparta

MEDITERRANEAN SEA

Knossos •

GREEK LANDS

This map shows the land of Greece. The Greeks lived on the mainland and on the many islands in the Aegean Sea. To the East can be seen some of the Greek cities on the coast of Asia Minor, which was known as Ionia.

	2000 BC	1800 BC	1500 BC	1200 BC	1000 BC
EVENTS IN GREECE	Civilization of the Minoans in Crete, centered on the royal palaces such as Knossos.	Mycenaean people grow in power. They trade all over the Mediterranean sea. The graves of their chieftains are full of treasure.	Fall of the Minoan capital at Knossos, Crete. Fall of the Mycenaeans.	Phoenicians spread throughout Mediterranean. Some Greeks flee to Asia Minor and establish towns there.	Iron introduced.
PERIOD IN WESTERN HISTORY	Bronze age c. 2900–1000 BC				Dark Age c. 1100–800 BC
EVENTS IN BRITAIN	Stonehenge built in Britain.				
EVENTS AROUND THE WORLD	Indus Valley civilizations in Pakistan. Rise of Babylon.		Period of Egyptian New Kingdom. Hittite Empire reaches its height in Asia.		

Minoan script disc

Mycenaean pot

Egyptian head

800 BC	600 BC	500 BC	400 BC	200 BC
Ionian and Black Sea colonies founded by Greeks. Greek alphabet invented. Homer's poems the *Iliad* and *Odyssey* composed. First Olympic Games in 776 BC	Coins introduced in Greece. People of Sparta control the Peloponnese peninsula, south of the Greek mainland. Democracy, a new system of government, begins in Athens.	Persian invasions begin. Athens reaches its peak of power. Greatest cultural flowering in Athens, known as the Age of Pericles. The Parthenon is built on the Acropolis.	Rise of Macedonia, northern Greece. Fall of Spartan power. Alexander the Great, King of Macedonia, leads military campaigns in Asia.	Macedonia becomes a province of the Roman Empire, bringing an end to Greek power.
Archaic period c. 800–500 BC		Classical period c.500–336 BC		

Homer

Alexander the Great

Hellenistic period c.323–30 BC

The Parthenon

800 BC	600 BC	500 BC	400 BC	200 BC
Rise of Etruscan civilization in Italy. City of Rome founded in 735 BC. Chou dynasty rules in China. Assyrian Empire established. Olmec civilization appears in Mexico.	In China, the philosopher Confucius is born. Assyrians conquer Lower Egypt. Rise of the Persian Empire. Celtic peoples arrive in south-east England.	Persian king Darius invades Greece. First copper used in Africa.	Maya civilization emerging in Central America c. 300 BC.	Roman armies invade Britain. Egypt becomes a Roman province. Great Wall of China built in 221 BC.

THE LEGEND OF TROY

There is a time of which we know comparatively little in Greek history, the Dark Age. Stories of adventure have come down to us from this time, the most famous of which are the *Iliad* and the *Odyssey*, composed by a poet called Homer.

The *Iliad* is about a great city called Troy, in Asia Minor, which was attacked by the Greeks. Greek soldiers managed to get inside Troy by a clever trick – they made a big wooden horse which they left outside the walls of the city. The inquisitive Trojans dragged the horse into the city and later that night Greek soldiers, hidden inside the horse, crept out and captured Troy.

PERIODS OF GREEK HISTORY

c. 2900–1000 BC
The Bronze Age

c. 1100–800 BC
The Dark Age

c. 800–500 BC
The Archaic Period

c. 500–336 BC
The Classical Period

c. 336–30 BC
The Hellenistic Period

WHERE·DID THE·GREEKS GET·THEIR ·FOOD?·

The people of ancient Greece grew most of their own food. There were many small farms in the countryside where wheat and barley were grown for bread and porridge. Other important crops were peas and beans, and fruits such as grapes, olives, pears, pomegranates and apples. Plows were sometimes made out of the curved branch of a tree which was dragged through the soil by an ox. The sower would follow the plowman and scatter the seeds in his footsteps. At harvest time, in May, the farmers would cut the corn with sharp sickles.

OLIVE GROVES
On the vase to the left you can see some men picking olives. One of them sits in the tree and shakes the branches while others gather the olives in baskets. If you go to Greece today you can still see olive groves almost everywhere. The trees flourish in the dry, rocky soils of Greece, especially near the city of Athens. The fruit of the olive is crushed to make olive oil for use in cooking. The Greeks also used olive oil instead of soap to clean themselves and for their little clay lamps, which provided the main form of light in homes.

FARM ANIMALS
Horses were reared in rich pastures, but this land was rare so only the well-off could afford it. The land was also too dry for the grazing of cattle and sheep on a large scale. Oxen, mules and donkeys were used for pulling plows and carts. Pigs and poultry were kept to provide luxury foods at dinner parties. Goats were the most common farm animals. They could live in very dry areas, they provided milk and cheese and even their skins.

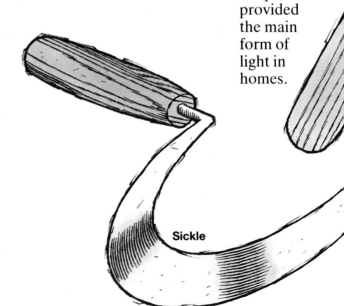

Sickle

12

Bill hook

Pick-axe

HUNTING

Rich young men probably ate more meat than other people because they could afford to go hunting on horseback. Carrying their long hunting spears, they caught wild boar, deer and hare, as well as birds such as swans, geese, thrushes and nightingales. The huntsman below returns with his catch – a fox and a hare.

FISHING

Fish was usually the main course at dinner time. Wooden fishing boats, nets and fishing spears were used to catch tuna, mackerel, sturgeon, shellfish, squid and octopus. The seas around Greece were teeming with fish.

FOOD AND THE GODS

Some foods were associated with particular gods. The olive tree was so greatly prized by the Athenians that they thought it came from the goddess Athena herself. The Greeks believed she struck the rock of the Acropolis with her spear and the first olive tree sprouted there.

Wine was drunk at the festivals of Dionysus, the god of wine. Cakes were also offered to him.

The pomegranate fruit was a symbol of death and the Underworld, the world of the dead. This was because the goddess Persephone had eaten six pomegranate seeds while in the Underworld (see page 28).

13

Breakfast and lunch were light meals – usually bread dipped in wine and water followed by dried figs, olives and perhaps some cheese. The main meal was in the evening. Food was eaten raw, boiled or roasted. The Greeks used their fingers or a knife and spoon. There were no forks. They had no potatoes, rice or sugar and so fewer people would have been overweight. Instead of sugar they used honey.

A DRINKING PARTY

Men held drinking parties (*symposia*) where slaves served food on little tables placed in front of the couches. A favorite pastime was the game of *kottabos*, shown on this vase on the left. Each player would flick the dregs of his wine at a target and bet on who would hit the mark.

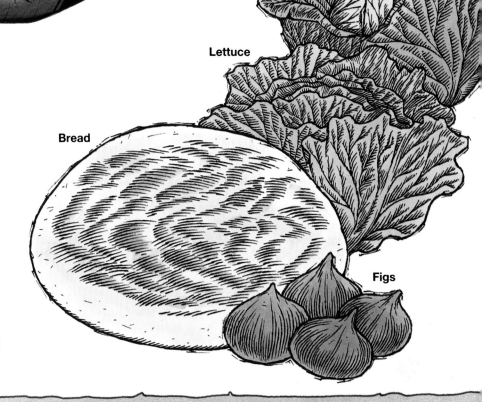

Cabbage

Lettuce

Bread

Figs

PARTY FOOD

Many different courses were served at the *symposion*. Slaves would serve exotic little dishes of jellyfish, pine nuts, celery, dates and oysters all mixed up together. Then there was the main course, usually fish flavored with herbs such as oregano and bay, and side dishes of vineleaves and fennel. The main course was followed by nuts, figs, grapes, cheeses and cakes sweetened with fruit and honey. Most people ate meat only on special days, but they had plenty of fish, fruit and vegetables.

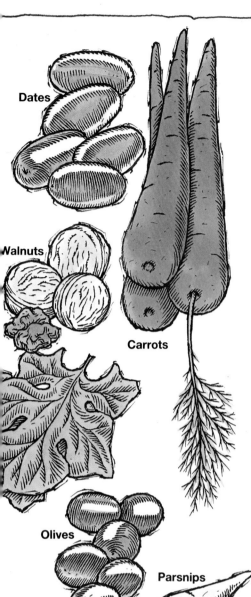

Dates

Walnuts

Carrots

Olives

Parsnips

Grapes

FISH DISH

A number of plates painted with pictures of fish like the one on the right have been found. They have a hollow in the middle, probably to hold a thick sauce in which the banqueter would dip his piece of fish before eating it. Fish was one of the commonest foods, as the supply was so plentiful.

CUPS, JUGS AND BOWLS

Most of the pots which you can see today in museums were used as containers for food and wine.

The Greeks always mixed their wine with water in a big mixing bowl called a *krater*.

Young boys would dip jugs, called *oinochoe*, into the *krater* to fill the large drinking cups.

A *hydria* or water pot has three handles. The *amphora*, for wine or oil, has two.

DRINKING TOO MUCH

Women were not invited as guests to the *symposion*, but they were sometimes there to serve the wine and to entertain the men. On this vase a girl holds a young man's head while he is being sick after drinking too much wine.

DID·THE GREEKS·HAVE· FAMILIES LIKE·OURS?

Ancient Greek writers describe family life mainly in Athens. Families were generally bigger than ours. Parents and children lived together with other relatives, for example elderly parents, and widowed and unmarried aunts. There might also be young cousins, perhaps the children of an uncle who had been killed in battle or of an aunt who had died in childbirth. The head of the family, the father, had complete control.

CHILDBIRTH

Many women died while giving birth. Here you can see a grave *stele*, a carved stone made for the grave of a young mother. The mother is seated. In front of her is a child and a slave girl holding out a box of jewelery. Such tomb reliefs are quite common, and occasionally have tender inscriptions on them from the grieving husband.

WOMEN AT WORK

Women were usually much younger than their husbands. They spent most of their time indoors looking after the children, supervising slaves, spinning and weaving. They are nearly always shown, on Greek vases, busy at their houshold tasks and rarely in the company of their husbands. Women of high status only went out with an escort.

Women had very little power outside the home. They were expected to look after the family and have children. In Athens wives and citizens could not own property or money, but foreign women in Athens could.

DOLLS

Greek children must have had soft toys made of fabric and stuffed with straw, but these have not survived. Their clay dolls, like the one on the right, looked like puppets as they had jointed arms and legs. Over time, this one has faded, but originally it would have had a painted face and brightly colored clothes. Clay dolls kneading dough or sitting on chairs have been found in the graves of little girls. They may have been tokens of their lost lives.

Babies who lived for more than ten days were formally given their names and were welcomed into their family with celebrations.

When children reached the age of twelve or thirteen they stopped playing with their toys and at a temple ceremony dedicated them to the gods as a sign of leaving childhood behind. Soon after this the girls would get married. Men did not marry until later.

Here is a dedication to a goddess:
"Maiden goddess, to you before her marriage, Timarete gives
Her cap, her tambourine, her favorite ball
And as is proper, O Artemis,
her childhood toys, her dolls, her all."

GAMES AND TOYS

Greek children played ball games, including a game like hockey. They also had bowling hoops and spinning tops. Small children had clay rattles in the shape of pigs or owls which are illustrated below. They had hobby-horses and miniature ox-carts or horse-drawn carts. Both children and adults enjoyed board games like draughts. Clay and bone counters have survived from these games. They were believed to have originated in Asia Minor. A favorite game was knucklebones, a game of luck using the bones of small animals. You can read more about knucklebones on page 24.

LOVE AND WAR

On the drinking cup above, a woman fills the man's cup with wine. It is a farewell drink before he goes away to battle. She may not see him again. He is dressed in armor and she holds his shield in her left hand. The warrior is called Chrysippos and the girl is Zeuxo. Such tender departure scenes were common on vases because battles between the city-states happened frequently. Women had to get used to men often being away.

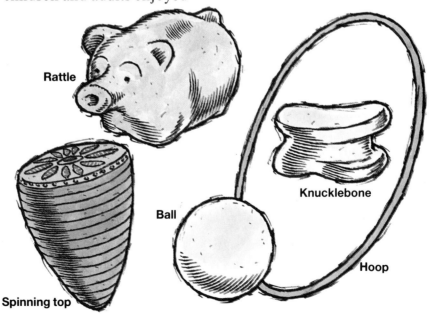

Rattle

Knucklebone

Ball

Hoop

Spinning top

When the Greeks built their temples, the houses for the gods, they made them out of solid stone and many of them survive today. However, their own homes, both in the towns and in the countryside, were made of mud bricks dried in the sun. For the foundations they used a layer of stones; the roofs were tiled. Inside there were tiny windows high up in the walls. The floors were made of beaten earth and covered with rush matting and rugs and walls were covered in colorful hangings.

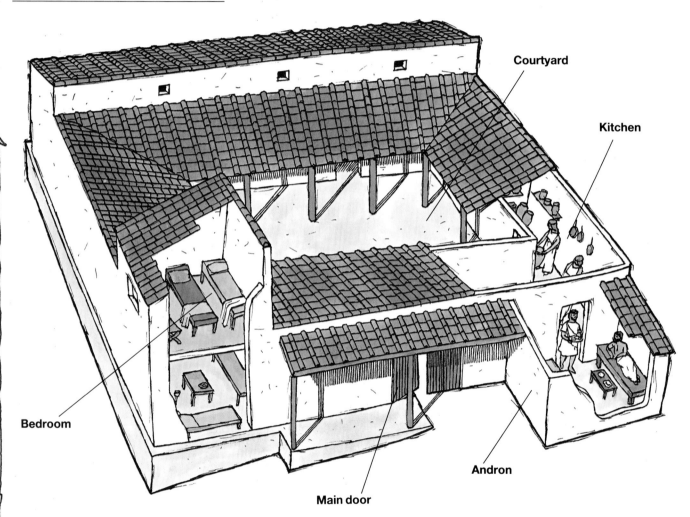

Courtyard

Kitchen

Bedroom

Andron

Main door

HOUSE PLAN

The rooms were arranged around a central courtyard, which was the heart of the household. Here there was an altar used for sacrifices to the gods. Children played in the courtyard and adults worked and gossipped in the sun. The number of rooms varied according to how rich the family was. Country farmhouses were bigger and had more land around the house to provide grazing for the goats and donkeys. There was a room where the women kept their looms and baskets of wool. Another room, the *andron*, was where the men of the house entertained their guests at the *symposion* (see page 14). It was full of cushions, couches and oil lamps.

A NEW HOME

On the vase below a young bride enters her new home through a doorway. She would have been welcomed in by her new mother-in-law and led to the hearth. Sweets and nuts were showered over her and her husband as a symbol of happiness and prosperity. Then the couple were led to their bedroom by the family and friends.

The Greeks had less furniture than we do today. They hung pots and other possessions on the walls instead of putting them in big cupboards. Women kept their personal possessions in baskets and small boxes. Tables and chairs were made of light wood which could be easily carried in and out of the house. They were often beautifully decorated with inlays of ivory, gold and silver.

There were two kinds of chair: a big high-backed chair with arms where the man of the house sat, called a *thronos*; and a smaller chair with curved legs called a *klismos*. Most people sat on stools which often had folding legs.

Couches for reclining on while eating looked much the same as beds. They were made of wood with a base of leather cords and covered with a mattress.

ROOM FOR DANCING

The vase on the right shows a young girl dancing in order to entertain a man who reclines on a couch covered with stripy cushions. She is playing a pair of castanets. To the right is a small table for food and wine. It was low enough to be pushed under the couch at the end of the meal. Greek tables were rectangular and they usually had three rather than four legs. Rooms used for entertainment had many brightly colored hangings and blankets which were woven by the women of the household.

DID·BOYS AND·GIRLS GO·TO ·SCHOOL?·

There were boys' schools in Athens and other towns. Reading, writing, public speaking, sports and music were taught to small classes of about seven or eight pupils. Learning by heart was thought to be very important and boys could often recite very long poems. From the age of about six the boy was taken to school by a family slave called a *paidogogos*. He stayed with the boy to make sure he behaved. Girls and poor children did not go to school.

WRITING TOOLS

At school the pupils wrote on papyrus scrolls using pens made from reeds. The papyrus plant came from Egypt and was very expensive. Ink was made from soot mixed with vegetable gum. They also wrote on wax tablets which were very useful for practicing on as they could be reused. Pupils wrote with a bronze tool called a *stylus* – the flat end was used for smoothing out mistakes.

Scroll

Reed pen

Bronze stylus

Papyrus

A GIRL'S EDUCATION

Girls stayed at home with their mothers and sisters and were taught the arts of spinning and weaving and running the household. Some of them learned to read and write. On this vase a girl is sitting down reading from a scroll. Other women are holding out household objects so that she can check them off against her list.

These are the letters of the
Greek alphabet.

A a	**B** b	**Γ** g	**Δ** d
E e	**Z** z	**H** EE/AY	**Θ** TH
I i	**K** k	**Λ** l	**M** m
N n	**Ξ** X/KS	**O** o	**Π** p
P r	**Σ** s	**T** t	**Y** U/OO
Φ F/PH	**X** CH	**Ψ** PS	**Ω** OH

MUSIC

Playing a musical instrument
was an important part of a boy's
education. Favorite instruments
were the lyre, the *kithara* and
the double pipes. The lyre had a
sound box made from the shell
from the shell of a tortoise. The
of a tortoise. The *kithara* was
bigger and made of wood. The
double pipes were also made of
wood and had a reed
mouthpiece. Unfortunately only
scraps of written music survive.

EXERCISE

Boys were also taught physical
exercise so that they would grow
up to be fit and strong soldiers.
On this drinking cup to the
right, a boy is shown
running along
with his hoop.
Youths were taught
dancing and athletics
by special teachers
called *paidotribes*.
There were training
grounds (*gymnasia*)
as well as wrestling
schools (*palaistrai*).
To the Greeks, physical
fitness was as important in the
boy's education as reading,
writing and arithmetic.
Philosophers would often come
to the *gymnasia* to teach the
pupils there.

WHO·WENT·TO·WORK·IN·GREEK·TIMES?

Most country people worked on the land. Farming was the most important work because it provided food. In the towns there were many trades and crafts. There were potters and bronze workers, sculptors and jewelers, cobblers and bakers. Lawyers, doctors and teachers also worked in big towns like Athens. Slaves did all the heavy work in households, but they were often treated kindly. Slaves who worked in the silver mines at Laurion in Attica, however, led very hard lives and were sometimes made to wear leg-irons to stop them escaping.

BAKING

Look at this clay model of a woman kneading dough on a special work table. She might be a slave making the bread for a family. When it was new this figure would have been brightly colored, but the paint has faded.

HOUSEWORK

On the vase above the mistress of the house hands her slave girl a big bundle of pink cloth. Notice how the lady has her hair elegantly piled up on top of her head with a diadem in it. The slave girl has short cropped hair and stands ready to receive the material.

Women produced all the cloth needed for the clothes and furnishings in the home. Rich ladies were confined to the house and had very little freedom. Poorer women might sell their weaving in the *agora*, the market place.

CRAFTSMEN AT WORK

On the right a carpenter is using a drill while making a piece of furniture. Fine woodwork does not survive because wood decays so quickly. But many objects made of marble and metal have survived. Stone sculptors worked with chisels and mallets, and they painted the finished statues in bright colors. Bronze was used not only for statues but also for everyday objects such as lamps and horse harnesses.

MAKING CLOTH

Women spent much of their time spinning and weaving. The fleece was first cleaned and dyed and then it was ready to be spun into yarn. They used a distaff and spindle made of wood or bronze to tease out the fibers and twist them. The the yarn was woven on a loom, which leaned against a wall. One set of threads called the weft runs across the loom. The other set, known as the warp, hangs down from the crossbar on top.

Loom

Spindle

Distaff

SLAVES

Slaves in Greece were used as servants and laborers. They had no legal rights. Slaves were usually prisoners of war – non-Greek peoples from the fringes of the Greek world. Men, women and children were sold into slavery. But a few slaves could be paid for their work and might even save up and buy their freedom.
By the fifth century BC there may have been 100,000 slaves in Attica, the region around Athens. This was twice the number of free citizens.
Slaves who had to work in the silver mines often had to lie on their backs for ten hours at a time, chiselling out the ore from the seam above them.

WHAT·DID THE·GREEKS DO·IN·THEIR SPARE·TIME?

The Greeks stopped work when there was a festival in honor of a god or goddess. In Athens the festival of Athena was a public holiday. Various festivals of Dionysus took place during the year and were celebrated with much drinking of wine and dancing and singing. Some festivals were associated with games. The most important were the Olympic Games, held at Olympia in honor of Zeus, the king of all the gods. In the countryside, people also had parties and holidays at harvest-time and for weddings and birthdays.

FESTIVAL GAMES

On the left is a horse-racing scene painted on a special vase called a Panathenaic *amphora*. Such vases were given as prizes at the grand festival of Athena, which was held in Athens with special magnificence every four years. The victors at the games that formed part of the festival received these pots. They were filled with olive oil and always had, on one side, a painting of the event which had been won. On the other was a picture of Athena herself in all her military splendor.

KNUCKLEBONES

On the right is a lovely terracotta showing two women playing knucklebones. A Greek writer described the game as follows: *"The knucklebones are thrown into the air and an attempt is made to catch them on the back of the hand. If you are only partially successful you have to pick up the knucklebones which have fallen to the ground without letting fall those already on the hand."*

LONG JUMP

Another *amphora* shows an athlete in the long jump event, which was part of the ancient 'five events' (pentathlon). The man with the stick is the umpire or the trainer. The athlete is holding a pair of jumping weights, which he swings behind him to help him jump further. The jumping weights were made of lead or stone.

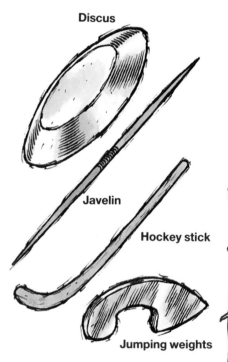

Discus

Javelin

Hockey stick

Jumping weights

FAVORITE GAMES

Popular games included:

Running
Horse-racing
Chariot-racing
Boxing
Wrestling
Discus
Javelin
Long jump

The discus and javelin were used in throwing competitions.

The *pankration* was a cross between boxing and wrestling, with almost anything allowed except for gouging the eyes, or biting or breaking the fingers of your opponent.

CRUEL SPORTS

Sometimes the Greeks amused themselves with cruel games. For example, here on a carved relief you can see spectators enjoying a fight between a dog and a cat. Cock-fighting was also quite popular, but on the whole the Greeks did not like spectator sports involving cruelty to animals. They preferred other sports, and they loved music, poetry, and telling riddles.

WHAT·DID·THE·GREEKS·WEAR?

Greek clothes were loosely draped around the body and held together with pins and brooches. They were made of finely spun wool or linen and were cool to wear in the hot climate. Men, women and children were similarly dressed. The main garment was a tunic called a *chiton* and a big oblong cloak, a *himation*, for outdoor use. The clothes were often dyed bright colors: pink, blue, purple or saffron yellow. Sandals were worn outdoors and boots for walking or riding in the country. Country people also wore goatskins to keep themselves warm.

FASHIONABLE WOMEN

This terracotta figurine shows two beautifully dressed ladies having a whispered conversation. They are wearing the *chiton* and *himation*. The woman on the left is probably a married woman as she wears her *himation* pulled up to cover her head. The other woman has her hair piled up in fashionable waves and held in place with a hairband. Rich women might even be able to afford silk, which was available by the fourth century BC.

JEWELERY

Rich ladies wore plenty of jewelery. Made of gold and silver, it was often exquisitely decorated with tiny gold granules and thin gold wire. In later times, jewels such as amethysts and emeralds were imported from the East to make necklaces and diadems.

WEDDING SCENE

On the vase to the right a young bride is being prepared for her wedding. She sits on a chair while her sisters and friends bring her jewelery to her. On the wall behind hangs a mirror. Pots like this were often given as presents as containers for perfume and cosmetics.

MEN'S CLOTHES

Young men sometimes wore only the *himation*, without the tunic beneath. It was wrapped around the body with one end thrown over the shoulder. The man below comes from a vase painting. You can see how graceful his cloak could look. It was very important that it should hang perfectly, so its edge was sometimes weighted with little clay balls.

A shorter cloak, a *chlamys*, was used for riding or hunting. It was fastened on the shoulder with a brooch.

 TUNIC STYLES

There were two different kinds of tunic. The earliest was the Doric *peplos*, a woollen tunic worn only by women and fastened at the shoulders with long pins. It had an overfold at the top. The Ionic *chiton*, worn by both men and women, was made of finely spun wool or linen. It had no overfold and was arranged on the shoulders to form loose, elbow-length sleeves.

A belt was tied around the waist of both the *peplos* and the *chiton*. The belt was worn high or low on the body according to the changing fashion.

Ionic *chiton*

Doric *peplos*

WHO·DID THE·GREEKS ·WORSHIP?·

Ordinary life and religion were closely linked in the Greek world. The Greeks worshipped many gods and goddesses and they believed in evil spirits too. Worshippers hoped that the gods would treat them well as long as they offered them the right prayers or animal sacrifice, or agricultural products like wheatcakes. The most important gods were thought to live on Mount Olympus. They were known by all the Greeks and had great temples dedicated to them.

PERSEPHONE

On the left is Persephone, daughter of Demeter, both goddesses concerned with fertility of the earth. Persephone had been stolen from her mother and carried off to the Underworld. While she was there, she ate some pomegranate seeds, the food of the dead. From then on she had to spend part of every year in the Underworld. This time represented winter in the Greek world.

ZEUS AND ATHENA

On the vase above the painter shows the birth of the goddess Athena. She was born from the head of her father Zeus. Zeus is sitting on his throne holding his thunderbolt. You can see the top half of Athena coming out of his head. She is dressed as a goddess of war, wearing a helmet and holding a shield. To the right stands Hephaestus, the smith god, who is holding an axe with which he cracked open Zeus's head so that Athena could be born.

HERACLES

The dramatic scene on this vase shows the hero, Heracles, fighting with a sea monster. The monster is a Triton, a dangerous son of Poseidon, god of the sea. It is half-fish and half-human – notice his long, forked and scaly tail. In the myths of ancient Rome, the same hero appears again. The Romans called him Hercules.

DELPHI

On the right is a view of some of the buildings which survive today at the site of Delphi. This famous shrine was dedicated mainly to the worship of Apollo. (Temples to the goddess Athena have also been found in the area.) Apollo was the god of music, light and healing and he appears in Greek art as a beautiful young man. The oracle at Delphi is the most famous in Greece. Here, the god was thought to speak through his priestess, Pythia. Officials of the Greek city-states came to ask the god's advice on political matters.

THE FAMILY OF GODS

There were many Greek gods. Those who lived on Mount Olympus were known as the Olympians. King of the gods was Zeus (1), shown in Greek art as a mature bearded man, holding a thunderbolt. His wife was the goddess Hera (2). His brother Poseidon ruled the sea (he carried a trident or fishing spear). Another brother was Pluto, king of the Underworld. Other gods included Ares (war 3), Aphrodite (love and beauty), Athena (wisdom and warfare 4), and Artemis, the huntress goddess. Dionysos was god of wine and fertility.

Hermes was a messenger god and the patron of travelers. Hestia was goddess of the hearth (5).

DID·THE GREEKS·GO ·TO·THE· DOCTOR?

The Greeks thought that sickness and disease were punishments sent by the gods, so they asked the gods for help to cure them. They went specially to the god of medicine, Asclepius. His most famous temple was at Epidaurus, where sick people came in large numbers. They were looked after by the priests of Asclepius who treated them when they were asleep and prescribed diets, exercise and baths. A more scientific kind of medicine was practiced by a doctor called Hippocrates. He set out the methods a doctor should follow.

BATTLEWOUND
One the vase above a doctor binds up the arm of a young boy. He may have taken blood from his patient, a common practice because blood was thought to contain the disease. Perhaps the arm had been wounded in battle.

OFFERINGS
Patients often used terracotta or bronze models to show which part of their body was sick. Bronze versions were made as offerings. Models of legs, eyes, ears, breasts and noses have been found at shrines.

SURGICAL INSTRUMENTS

Surgical instruments were made of bronze and iron. They included forceps, knives and probes. With all these, physicians operated on the different parts of the body, using opium and the root of the mandrake, (a powerful herb), as anaesthetics. These were not very effective and operations must always have been painful and very dangerous.

Surgical instruments

MIRACLE CURES

Many types of illness were 'cured' by the god Asclepius. Sometimes the cures were more like miracles. One patient called Phalysios, who was blind, was given a special tablet to look at. As he read the tablet his sight came back, but to his horror he found that he was reading an order to him to give a very expensive gift to the temple. Belief in Asclepius was strong, and continued well into Roman times.

ASCLEPIUS

To the right is a sculpture of the god Asclepius. According to legend he was the son of Apollo, and was brought up by a centaur (a creature who was half man and half horse) who taught him the art of medicine. He has a beard and a kind and serious face and holds a long stick, around which curls a snake, the symbol of medicine.

WHO·RULED ·THE· GREEKS?

Greece was made up of independent city-states. In early times these were ruled by rich landowners and powerful leaders called tyrants. The tyrants were driven out by the people and a new form of government was established, called democracy. In the modern world, democracy means everyone has a vote. In ancient Athens only citizens were allowed to vote. Many people, including women, slaves and foreigners, were not citizens.

ALEXANDER THE GREAT

In 336 BC Alexander became King of Macedonia in the north-east of Greece. He was a very successful soldier and through his military conquests built up a huge empire and became known as Alexander the Great. He defeated the Persians and captured territories in Asia Minor, Egypt and India. These conquests were responsible for spreading Greek culture far beyond the land of Greece. This bronze statuette of Alexander is a Roman copy of an earlier Greek original showing him on horseback leading his troops into battle.

PERICLES

Here is a Roman marble bust of Pericles, the great leader and *strategos* of Athens from 443 to 429 BC. His democratic policies and his great pride in his city won him the whole-hearted support of the people. He is famous for reconstructing magnificent buildings on the Acropolis, which were destroyed by the Persians.

POLITICAL EXILE

The Athenians had a way of getting rid of politicians they did not like. At the Assembly people would write the name of the politician on pieces of pot (*ostrakon*) shown in the illustration below. In the scene above a number of Greeks are casting their votes (pieces of pot) and are watched by Athena and other gods. If there was a large enough vote against the man he would be exiled from Athens for ten years.

Ostrakon

 THE ASSEMBLY

Every citizen had the right to speak at the Assembly in Athens. It met on a hill called the Pnyx. Meetings were huge – at least 6000 people gathered there every 10 days. If numbers were low, the police went out into the streets to round up the citizens. One famous Athenian orator, Demosthenes, who had to speak at the Assembly, is said to have cured himself of stammering by practicing talking with a mouthful of pebbles. He also taught himself to speak very loudly by yelling on the seashore against the noise of the breaking waves.

WERE·THE GREEKS ·ARTISTS?·

Greek civilization is famous for the beauty of its art. Temples and sanctuaries were adorned with marble and bronze statues of gods and goddesses. Artists worked also in precious metals such as ivory, gold and silver, making precious jewelery and figures. Even everyday things like pots were beautifully painted with human and animal figures, and geometric and plant designs. The human figure was one of their favorite subjects.

AN ATHLETE
On the left is a statue of a young man. He may have been a famous athlete made to resemble the god Apollo. He was carved in 490 BC in Athens. The sculptor has carved his curly hair in solid marble, and there are holes in his head where a metal headband was once fixed. Greek artists liked to show their skill in carving or painting the muscles of the human body.

VASE PAINTING
The vase above is painted in the red-figure style. The artist has shown details of the ship and the figures by painting lines of different thickness and shades of black. The picture shows an adventure of Odysseus, who was warned about the terrible Sirens, half-bird, half-female creatures. They lived on a rocky shore and sang so beautifully that passing sailors were tempted overboard to join them and were eaten.

POTTERY STYLES

On the left is a group of vases painted in different styles. They are covered with scenes from daily life and mythology. Because vases were placed in tombs they were not broken and often survive in excellent condition.

In the sixth century BC, vases were painted in the black-figure style, with figures painted in black and the background left in a reddish-brown color. Later, in the fifth century, the red-figure style took over and the background is black, with the figures in reddish brown. The lustrous black is thin clay paint made of the same red clay as the pot. It was painted on before firing and turned black while the pot was being fired.

VASE NAMES

Dinos Bowl for mixing wine and water.

Olpe Jug for wine.

Pyxis Cosmetic box.

Aryballos Perfume bottle.

Kylix Drinking cup.

Kantharos Drinking cup with two tall handles.

Loutrophoros Large vase for bringing water for the ritual bath of a bride.

STATUE OF A GOD

On the right is the bronze head from a statue of a god. The eyes were originally inlaid with glass or marble and even had bronze eyelashes. Not many large bronze statues have survived in one piece as they were often melted down in ancient times. Fortunately, the most famous Greek statues were copied by Roman sculptors in marble, and many of these Roman statues survive and can be seen in museums today.

DID·THE GREEKS GO·TO·THE ·THEATER?·

Going to a performance of drama was a normal part of Greek life. The plays were either tragedies or comedies. Religious plays were held in honor of Dionysus, the god of wine. A chorus of people dressed in costume recited poems and danced. Then individual actors were added, but the chorus remained to tell the story of the play. Greek plays were staged in open-air theaters. The audience sat on seats arranged around a circular space known as the *orchestra*. As theaters were usually built into hillsides, the seats rose in tiers giving good views all round.

Theatrical masks

MASKS
Actors wore masks made of stiffened linen or clay. Male and female parts were played by men, and they changed masks to move from one part to another. The large mouths of the masks amplified their voices.

OPEN-AIR THEATER
This is a photograph of a splendidly preserved theater at Dodona in northern Greece. It shows how huge numbers of people came to the theater. This one could have seated 14,000 spectators. It is built into the hillside and the seats rise naturally in tiers. Not only were the views good, but the sound from the stage was excellent. Important people such as foreign visitors sat at the front in specially reserved stone seats. The back wall of the stage was called the *skene*, which is where our word scenery comes from.

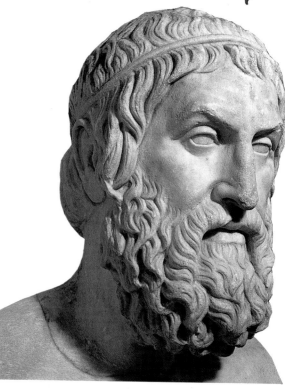

COMEDIES

Above is a scene from a comedy. The actors are wearing grotesque masks and tight-fitting costumes that were also padded to exaggerate their stomachs and bottoms for comic effect. Wigs and masks with hairstyles attached were also worn by the actors. Writers of comedy, of whom the most famous was Aristophanes, used ordinary characters to poke fun at politicians and intellectuals.

SOPHOCLES

The most famous authors of tragic plays were Aeschylus, Sophocles and Euripides. They wrote about the legendary kings and princes of a much earlier time in Greece. Above is a Roman portrait of Sophocles who was born about 496 BC. He wrote *King Oedipus, Antigone* and *Electra*.

 THEATER FACTS

Plays were put on at festival times in Athens. The male citizens of Athens made up most of the audience.

As the stone seats were very hard to sit on, people brought their own cushions with them.

Special effects were sometimes used in the theater. For example, pebbles were rolled on copper sheets to imitate the sound of thunder. Actors were sometimes hoisted into the air on a kind of crane.

WERE THE GREEKS SCIENTISTS?

The Greeks' skill in science and technology is most clearly seen in their temple architecture. Temples were usually made of marble or limestone which had to be brought from the quarry in waggons pulled by oxen.

In the Hellenistic period, a temple to the muses was built at Alexandria in Egypt. It had a large library which attracted scholars and scientists from all over the Greek world. A lot of important research went on there and cog-wheels, steam engines and slot-machines were made. However, few of them were put to any practical use.

TEMPLE BUILDING

Raising massive temples of marble and other stone required great skill as well as hard labor. The columns that formed a tall colonnade around the building were made up of massive cylinders of stone. These were held together with metal pegs. The stones were lifted into place using ropes and pulleys. The building of the temple amounted to a major engineering project.

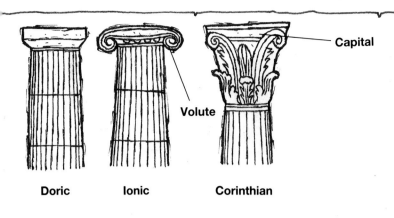

Doric   Ionic   Corinthian

Capital

Volute

ARCHITECTURAL STYLES

In Greek temple architecture there were two main styles, the Doric and the Ionic. The Doric was popular in mainland Greece. The capitals, the tops of the columns, were plain. In the eastern parts of Greece and the islands the Ionic style was more common. The columns were thinner and the capitals were decorated with volutes, scroll-like forms carved into the four corners of the block of stone. The Corinthian capital had carvings in the shape of acanthus leaves. These often appear on Roman buildings too.

PYTHAGORAS

Greek scholars such as Pythagoras, Euclid and Archimedes, worked out some basic rules of mathematics. Pythagoras's theorem on triangles is still used in geometry today. He came from the island of Samos in eastern Greece – an area which produced a number of other famous scientists and thinkers. They were strongly influenced by the ancient cultures of Babylon and Egypt.

 SCIENTISTS

The astronomer Aristarchus discovered that the earth moved round the sun.

Another astronomer, Anaxagoras, realized that the moon's light is reflected from the sun.

The scientist Xenophanes understood that fossils were the remains of plant and animal life in rocks.

An astronomer called Hipparchus located 850 stars.

In medicine, Herophilus began dissecting bodies and learned about the nervous system.

ARCHIMEDES

The Hellenistic inventor Archimedes built a device for raising water from one level to another which is now known as the Archimedes screw. As the screw was turned the water rose. Pumps like this are still in use in Africa today.

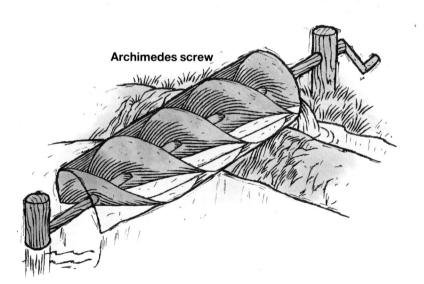

Archimedes screw

DID·THE GREEKS·GO ON·LONG JOURNEYS?

Greece is a mountainous country and, even today, it is difficult to take long journeys by road. People often used the sea. They sailed in wooden ships, often sticking close to the shore in case of sudden storms or pirate attacks. People traveled far to take part in games and festivals, but trade was the main reason for traveling between the Greek mainland and the islands. Slow heavy merchant ships could travel long distances. Greek warships were faster, being longer and lower in the water. These were known as triremes.

MERCHANTS AND PIRATES

This vase has a vivid illustration of the dangers of sailing the high seas. A merchant ship has just been rammed by a fast pirate ship with a pointed prow, specially strengthened for the purpose.

The cargo will be taken on board their own ship by the pirates who will then sail away leaving the merchant ship to sink and its crew to drown.

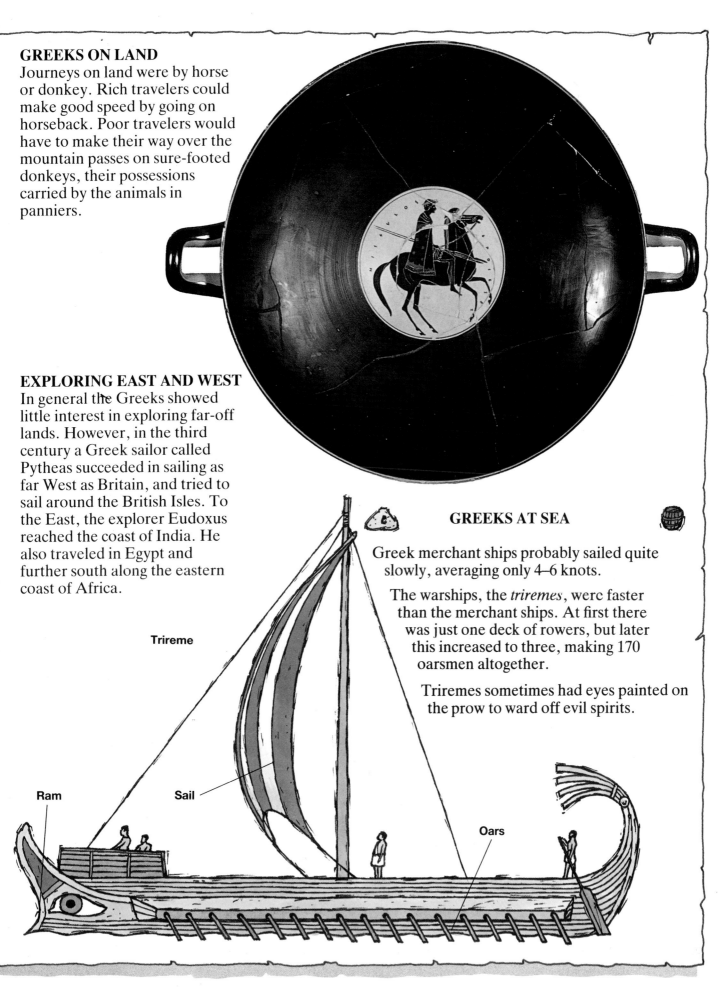

GREEKS ON LAND

Journeys on land were by horse or donkey. Rich travelers could make good speed by going on horseback. Poor travelers would have to make their way over the mountain passes on sure-footed donkeys, their possessions carried by the animals in panniers.

EXPLORING EAST AND WEST

In general the Greeks showed little interest in exploring far-off lands. However, in the third century a Greek sailor called Pytheas succeeded in sailing as far West as Britain, and tried to sail around the British Isles. To the East, the explorer Eudoxus reached the coast of India. He also traveled in Egypt and further south along the eastern coast of Africa.

GREEKS AT SEA

Greek merchant ships probably sailed quite slowly, averaging only 4–6 knots.

The warships, the *triremes*, were faster than the merchant ships. At first there was just one deck of rowers, but later this increased to three, making 170 oarsmen altogether.

Triremes sometimes had eyes painted on the prow to ward off evil spirits.

Trireme

Ram

Sail

Oars

Many Greek men had to join the army in time of war and had to pay for their own armor and weapons. The foot soldier in the army was called a *hoplite* because the Greek word for his round bronze shield was *hoplon*. He wore body armor and 'greaves' made of leather or metal to protect his legs. He fought with spear and sword in a close formation called a *phalanx*. The *phalanx* moved slowly on the battle field, but proved a very successful method of fighting. By the fourth century the Greek generals were also using archers and slingers.

HELMET

Here is a surviving helmet of the type known as Corinthian. It has a long distinctive nose piece and cheek guards. Helmets varied in shape. Some kinds had horse-hair crests.

ARMOR

Below is a *hoplite* wearing his armor. The body armor or 'cuirass' is made of bronze and leather. Earlier ones were made of two bronze plates fastened at the sides with straps. The round shield could be decorated with various emblems.

Helmet

Cuirass

Shield

Spear

Greaves

AT BATTLE
Scenes of fighting from Greek legend can often be seen on Greek vases. Below the Greek hero Achilles kills an Amazon warrior queen called Penthesilea. His spear is piercing her throat, but as she falls dying to the ground he falls in love with her.

SPARTAN SOLDIER
This bronze figure of a Spartan soldier on the right dates from the fifth century BC. Spartan soldiers wore scarlet cloaks to battle. They were well known for their bravery. Devoting their whole lives to soldiering, they spent most of their time in service and only occasionally visited their families.

ARCHER
On this Athenian cup below an archer from Scythia draws an arrow from a quiver while holding his bow with the other hand. Archers and stone-slingers formed the back-up troops of the Greek armies. Poorer men who could not afford the full *hoplite* armor joined these units.

SPARTA

The city of Sparta in the Peloponnese was the great enemy of Athens and her rival in power. By the fifth century BC, Sparta had become the strongest military power in Greece. Life in Sparta was dedicated to military service. Little boys lived at home with their parents only until the age of seven. After that they went to live in barracks with other boys and trained as soldiers. They had plain food and simple clothing and competed with each other to see who could endure the most flogging. Their land was farmed for them by *helots*, slaves who had been the free inhabitants of areas conquered by Sparta.

·GLOSSARY·

ACROPOLIS The Greek word means 'high city'. It was a fortified citadel where citizens could hide in time of war. The most famous acropolis was at Athens.

AGORA The market place of a Greek town, an open space with public buildings and temples.

AMPHORA A large two-handled clay pot to contain wine or oil.

ANDRON Dining room in a private house, used only by the men of the family.

ASSEMBLY Meeting of citizens to discuss the affairs of the city-state.

BLACK-FIGURE POTTERY Made in Athens especially in the sixth century BC. The figures stand out against a reddish background.

CAPITAL The carved top of a stone column. The three main types were the Doric, Ionic and Corinthian orders.

CHITON A tunic made of wool or linen worn by men and women.

CITY-STATE A town and the farmland around it.

DEMOCRACY Form of government by which power belongs to the people. The word is made up from two Greek words meaning 'people' and 'power'. Many Greek city-states had a democracy, but the most famous was Athens in the fifth century BC.

DIADEM A hair decoration, often made of gold and resembling a crown.

HELOTS Slaves of the Spartans who worked on the land.

HIMATION A woollen cloak.

HOPLITES Foot soldiers armed with spears and round shields who fought shoulder to shoulder.

KRATER A type of large bowl or vase used for mixing wine and water.

MUSES Greek gods of poetry, literature, music and dance.

ORACLES Places where the gods were believed to speak to human beings. The most famous was that of Apollo at Delphi.

PENTATHLON A contest of five events: running, jumping, throwing the discus and the javelin, and wrestling.

PEPLOS A woollen robe for women made from a single length of cloth.

PHALANX The battle formation used by *hoplites*. They stood shoulder to shoulder and in a block sometimes several rows deep.

RED-FIGURE POTTERY Made in Athens from the late fifth century onwards. Figures are in red against a dark background.

STELE A stone slab often put up over a grave and beautifully carved.

STRATEGOS Athenian army commander. There were ten, elected annually.

TRIREME A long Greek warship with about 170 oars arranged in three decks. Its main weapon was the underwater ram at its bow.

TYRANNY Government by one person who is above the law.

UNDERWORLD An underground kingdom, sometimes known as Hades. The souls of the dead were thought to go there. The god Pluto was its king.

· I N D E X ·

Achilles 43
Acropolis 8, 11, 13, 33, 44
agora 22, 44
Alexander the Great 11, 32
Alexandria 38
alphabet 11, 21
amphora 15, 24, 25, 44
andron 18, 44
Apollo 29, 31, 34, 44
Archimedes 39
architecture 38–39
army 8, 42–43
art 8, 29, 34–35
Asclepius 30, 31
Asia Minor (Ionia) 8, 9, 11,
    17, 32
Assembly 33, 44
Athena 13, 24, 28, 29
Athens 9, 11, 34, 43,
    acropolis 44, festivals 24,
    37, olives 12, 13, people 8,
    16, 20, 22, 23, 32, 33
athletics 21, 25, 34
Attica 9, 22, 23

Babylon 10, 39
battles 17, 42, 43
Bronze Age 10, 11
brooch 26, 27
building 18, 38

capitals 39, 44
chiton 26, 27, 44
city-states 8, 17, 29, 32, 44
clothes 22, 26–27, 43
coinage 8, 11
cosmetics 27
craftsmen 22, 23
Crete 10

dancing 19, 21, 24, 36, 44
Dark Ages 10, 11
Delphi 9, 29, 44
democracy 11, 32–33, 44
diadem 26, 44
Dionysus 13, 24, 29, 36
Dodona 9, 36

Egypt 20, 32, 38, 39, 41
Epidaurus 9, 30
Euripedes 37

families 16–17, 20, 22
farming 12, 22
festivals 13, 24, 40
food 12–15, 19, 22
furniture 19, 23

games 14, 17, 24–25, 40
government 8, 32–33, 44
graves 10, 16, 17, 35, 44
gymnasia 21

Hellenistic Period 11, 38, 39
helots 43, 44
himation 26, 27, 44
Hippocrates 30
Homer 11
hoplites 42, 44

instruments, musical 21,
surgical 31

jewelery 22, 26

Knossos 9, 10
krater 15, 44

loom 18, 23

Macedonia 11, 32
medicine 30–31, 39
Mediterranean 8, 10
Mount Olympus 9, 28, 29
muses 38, 44
music 8, 20, 21, 25, 29, 44
Mycenaeans 10

Odysseus 34
olive oil 12, 13, 14, 24
Olympia 9, 24
Olympic Games 11, 24
oracle 29, 44
orchestra 36

paidogogos 20

papyrus 20
Parthenon 11
pentathlon 25, 44
peplos 27, 44
Pericles 11, 33
Persephone 13, 28
Persians 11, 32, 33
phalanx 42, 44
Pluto 29, 44
Poseidon 9, 29
pottery 15, 22, 34–35
Pythagoras 39

religion 9, 28–29, 36
Roman Empire 11

sacrifice 18, 28
schools 20–21
science 38–39
sculptors 22, 23, 34, 35
slaves 14, 22–23, 32, 43,
family 16, 20, 22
soldiers 21, 32, 43, 44
Sophocles 37
Sparta 9, 11, 43
spinning 16, 20, 23
stele 16, 44
strategos 33, 44
stylus 20
symposia 14, 15, 18

technology 38–39
theater 36–37
toys 17
trade 8, 22, 40
travel 40–41
triremes 40, 41, 44
Troy 9, 11
tunic 26, 27, 44
tyrants 32, 44

Underworld 13, 28, 29, 44

weapons 10, 42, 44
weaving 16, 20, 23

Xenophanes 39

Zeus 24, 28, 29